GRANDFATHER MARTIN

By Wendy Orr

Illustrated by Kate Ellis

HOUGHTON MIFFLIN COMPANY
BOSTON
ATLANTA DALLAS GENEVA, ILLINOIS PALO ALTO PRINCETON

Grandfather Martin liked routine.

He also liked rules to follow,
things in their places, tidy houses,
clean shoes, and meals on time.

Grandmother Martin liked to do what she liked,

when she liked.

She liked to work in her garden,

read a book, or paint a picture,

and she did not care what time it was.

When Grandfather Martin was younger,

he worked in a big office with lots of other people.

He was always very busy.

Now Grandfather Martin did not go to work,

so he was not very busy.

One day Grandfather Martin watched

Grandmother Martin prepare dinner.

She went into the garden
to pick some carrots.
On the way she
pulled up some weeds,
patted the cat,
threw a ball for the dog,
picked some roses,
put them in a vase,
painted a picture,
and then went back to
pick the carrots.

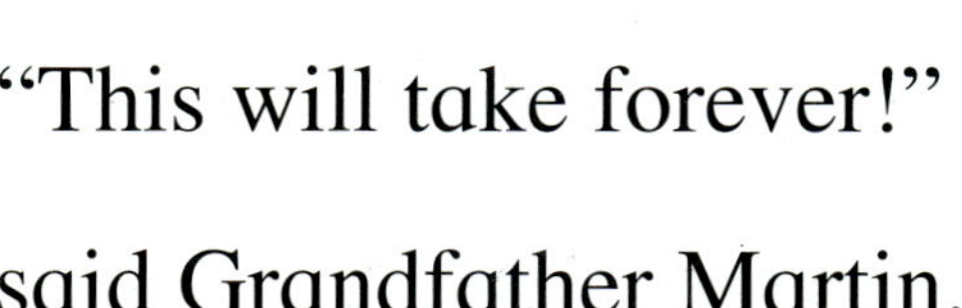

"This will take forever!"
said Grandfather Martin.

The next day at dinnertime he went out to the garden.

Grandmother Martin was building a birdhouse.

“It’s time to make dinner,” said Grandfather Martin.

“You make it tonight, dear,” said Grandmother Martin.

“I’m rather busy.”

Grandfather Martin went to the kitchen.

He did not know what to cook.

He did not know how to cook.

“How much of this?” he asked Grandmother Martin.

“How much of that?”

“A pinch of this,” said Grandmother Martin.

“A touch of that.”

“How long will it take?” asked Grandfather Martin.

“As long as it needs,” said Grandmother Martin.

This was not how Grandfather Martin liked to do things.

The next morning Grandfather Martin went shopping. He bought a cookbook, some measuring cups, some measuring spoons and a timer.

Now Grandfather Martin is a good cook.

And Grandmother Martin does what she likes,

when she likes.

And meals are always on time.